I
Can't
Remember

An Organizer For All Your
Passwords And Shit

WEBSITE:

USERNAME:

PASSWORD:

NOTES:

WEBSITE:

USERNAME:

PASSWORD:

NOTES:

WEBSITE:

USERNAME:

PASSWORD:

NOTES:

WEBSITE:

USERNAME:

PASSWORD:

NOTES:

WEBSITE:

USERNAME:

PASSWORD:

NOTES:

WEBSITE:

USERNAME:

PASSWORD:

NOTES:

WEBSITE:

USERNAME:

PASSWORD:

NOTES:

WEBSITE:

USERNAME:

PASSWORD:

NOTES:

WEBSITE:

USERNAME:

PASSWORD:

NOTES:

WEBSITE:

USERNAME:

PASSWORD:

NOTES:

WEBSITE:

USERNAME:

PASSWORD:

NOTES:

WEBSITE:

USERNAME:

PASSWORD:

NOTES:

WEBSITE:

USERNAME:

PASSWORD:

NOTES:

WEBSITE:

USERNAME:

PASSWORD:

NOTES:

WEBSITE:

USERNAME:

PASSWORD:

NOTES:

WEBSITE:

USERNAME:

PASSWORD:

NOTES:

WEBSITE:

USERNAME:

PASSWORD:

NOTES:

WEBSITE:

USERNAME:

PASSWORD:

NOTES:

WEBSITE:

USERNAME:

PASSWORD:

NOTES:

WEBSITE:

USERNAME:

PASSWORD:

NOTES:

WEBSITE:

USERNAME:

PASSWORD:

NOTES:

WEBSITE:

USERNAME:

PASSWORD:

NOTES:

WEBSITE:

USERNAME:

PASSWORD:

NOTES:

WEBSITE:

USERNAME:

PASSWORD:

NOTES:

WEBSITE:

USERNAME:

PASSWORD:

NOTES:

WEBSITE:

USERNAME:

PASSWORD:

NOTES:

WEBSITE:

USERNAME:

PASSWORD:

NOTES:

WEBSITE:

USERNAME:

PASSWORD:

NOTES:

WEBSITE:

USERNAME:

PASSWORD:

NOTES:

WEBSITE:

USERNAME:

PASSWORD:

NOTES:

WEBSITE:

USERNAME:

PASSWORD:

NOTES:

WEBSITE:

USERNAME:

PASSWORD:

NOTES:

WEBSITE:

USERNAME:

PASSWORD:

NOTES:

WEBSITE:

USERNAME:

PASSWORD:

NOTES:

WEBSITE:

USERNAME:

PASSWORD:

NOTES:

WEBSITE:

USERNAME:

PASSWORD:

NOTES:

WEBSITE:

USERNAME:

PASSWORD:

NOTES:

WEBSITE:

USERNAME:

PASSWORD:

NOTES:

WEBSITE:

USERNAME:

PASSWORD:

NOTES:

WEBSITE:

USERNAME:

PASSWORD:

NOTES:

WEBSITE:

USERNAME:

PASSWORD:

NOTES:

WEBSITE:

USERNAME:

PASSWORD:

NOTES:

WEBSITE:

USERNAME:

PASSWORD:

NOTES:

WEBSITE:

USERNAME:

PASSWORD:

NOTES:

WEBSITE:

USERNAME:

PASSWORD:

NOTES:

WEBSITE:

USERNAME:

PASSWORD:

NOTES:

WEBSITE:

USERNAME:

PASSWORD:

NOTES:

WEBSITE:

USERNAME:

PASSWORD:

NOTES:

WEBSITE:

USERNAME:

PASSWORD:

NOTES:

WEBSITE:

USERNAME:

PASSWORD:

NOTES:

WEBSITE:

USERNAME:

PASSWORD:

NOTES:

WEBSITE:

USERNAME:

PASSWORD:

NOTES:

WEBSITE:

USERNAME:

PASSWORD:

NOTES:

WEBSITE:

USERNAME:

PASSWORD:

NOTES:

WEBSITE:

USERNAME:

PASSWORD:

NOTES:

WEBSITE:

USERNAME:

PASSWORD:

NOTES:

WEBSITE:

USERNAME:

PASSWORD:

NOTES:

WEBSITE:

USERNAME:

PASSWORD:

NOTES:

WEBSITE:

USERNAME:

PASSWORD:

NOTES:

WEBSITE:

USERNAME:

PASSWORD:

NOTES:

WEBSITE:

USERNAME:

PASSWORD:

NOTES:

WEBSITE:

USERNAME:

PASSWORD:

NOTES:

WEBSITE:

USERNAME:

PASSWORD:

NOTES:

WEBSITE:

USERNAME:

PASSWORD:

NOTES:

WEBSITE:

USERNAME:

PASSWORD:

NOTES:

WEBSITE:

USERNAME:

PASSWORD:

NOTES:

WEBSITE:

USERNAME:

PASSWORD:

NOTES:

WEBSITE:

USERNAME:

PASSWORD:

NOTES:

WEBSITE:

USERNAME:

PASSWORD:

NOTES:

WEBSITE:

USERNAME:

PASSWORD:

NOTES:

WEBSITE:

USERNAME:

PASSWORD:

NOTES:

WEBSITE:

USERNAME:

PASSWORD:

NOTES:

WEBSITE:

USERNAME:

PASSWORD:

NOTES:

WEBSITE:

USERNAME:

PASSWORD:

NOTES:

WEBSITE:

USERNAME:

PASSWORD:

NOTES:

WEBSITE:

USERNAME:

PASSWORD:

NOTES:

WEBSITE:

USERNAME:

PASSWORD:

NOTES:

WEBSITE:

USERNAME:

PASSWORD:

NOTES:

WEBSITE:

USERNAME:

PASSWORD:

NOTES:

WEBSITE:

USERNAME:

PASSWORD:

NOTES:

WEBSITE:

USERNAME:

PASSWORD:

NOTES:

WEBSITE:

USERNAME:

PASSWORD:

NOTES:

WEBSITE:

USERNAME:

PASSWORD:

NOTES:

WEBSITE:

USERNAME:

PASSWORD:

NOTES:

WEBSITE:

USERNAME:

PASSWORD:

NOTES:

WEBSITE:

USERNAME:

PASSWORD:

NOTES:

WEBSITE:

USERNAME:

PASSWORD:

NOTES:

WEBSITE:

USERNAME:

PASSWORD:

NOTES:

WEBSITE:

USERNAME:

PASSWORD:

NOTES:

WEBSITE:

USERNAME:

PASSWORD:

NOTES:

WEBSITE:

USERNAME:

PASSWORD:

NOTES:

WEBSITE:

USERNAME:

PASSWORD:

NOTES:

WEBSITE:

USERNAME:

PASSWORD:

NOTES:

WEBSITE:

USERNAME:

PASSWORD:

NOTES:

WEBSITE:

USERNAME:

PASSWORD:

NOTES:

WEBSITE:

USERNAME:

PASSWORD:

NOTES:

WEBSITE:

USERNAME:

PASSWORD:

NOTES:

WEBSITE:

USERNAME:

PASSWORD:

NOTES:

WEBSITE:

USERNAME:

PASSWORD:

NOTES:

WEBSITE:

USERNAME:

PASSWORD:

NOTES:

WEBSITE:

USERNAME:

PASSWORD:

NOTES:

WEBSITE:

USERNAME:

PASSWORD:

NOTES:

WEBSITE:

USERNAME:

PASSWORD:

NOTES:

WEBSITE:

USERNAME:

PASSWORD:

NOTES:

WEBSITE:

USERNAME:

PASSWORD:

NOTES:

WEBSITE:

USERNAME:

PASSWORD:

NOTES:

WEBSITE:

USERNAME:

PASSWORD:

NOTES:

WEBSITE:

USERNAME:

PASSWORD:

NOTES:

WEBSITE:

USERNAME:

PASSWORD:

NOTES:

WEBSITE:

USERNAME:

PASSWORD:

NOTES:

WEBSITE:

USERNAME:

PASSWORD:

NOTES:

WEBSITE:

USERNAME:

PASSWORD:

NOTES:

WEBSITE:

USERNAME:

PASSWORD:

NOTES:

WEBSITE:

USERNAME:

PASSWORD:

NOTES:

WEBSITE:

USERNAME:

PASSWORD:

NOTES:

WEBSITE:

USERNAME:

PASSWORD:

NOTES:

WEBSITE:

USERNAME:

PASSWORD:

NOTES:

WEBSITE:

USERNAME:

PASSWORD:

NOTES:

WEBSITE:

USERNAME:

PASSWORD:

NOTES:

WEBSITE:

USERNAME:

PASSWORD:

NOTES:

WEBSITE:

USERNAME:

PASSWORD:

NOTES:

WEBSITE:

USERNAME:

PASSWORD:

NOTES:

WEBSITE:

USERNAME:

PASSWORD:

NOTES:

WEBSITE:

USERNAME:

PASSWORD:

NOTES:

WEBSITE:

USERNAME:

PASSWORD:

NOTES:

WEBSITE:

USERNAME:

PASSWORD:

NOTES:

WEBSITE:

USERNAME:

PASSWORD:

NOTES:

WEBSITE:

USERNAME:

PASSWORD:

NOTES:

WEBSITE:

USERNAME:

PASSWORD:

NOTES:

WEBSITE:

USERNAME:

PASSWORD:

NOTES:

WEBSITE:

USERNAME:

PASSWORD:

NOTES:

WEBSITE:

USERNAME:

PASSWORD:

NOTES:

WEBSITE:

USERNAME:

PASSWORD:

NOTES:

WEBSITE:

USERNAME:

PASSWORD:

NOTES:

WEBSITE:

USERNAME:

PASSWORD:

NOTES:

WEBSITE:

USERNAME:

PASSWORD:

NOTES:

WEBSITE:

USERNAME:

PASSWORD:

NOTES:

WEBSITE:

USERNAME:

PASSWORD:

NOTES:

WEBSITE:

USERNAME:

PASSWORD:

NOTES:

WEBSITE:

USERNAME:

PASSWORD:

NOTES:

WEBSITE:

USERNAME:

PASSWORD:

NOTES:

WEBSITE:

USERNAME:

PASSWORD:

NOTES:

WEBSITE:

USERNAME:

PASSWORD:

NOTES:

WEBSITE:

USERNAME:

PASSWORD:

NOTES:

WEBSITE:

USERNAME:

PASSWORD:

NOTES:

WEBSITE:

USERNAME:

PASSWORD:

NOTES:

WEBSITE:

USERNAME:

PASSWORD:

NOTES:

WEBSITE:

USERNAME:

PASSWORD:

NOTES:

WEBSITE:

USERNAME:

PASSWORD:

NOTES:

WEBSITE:

USERNAME:

PASSWORD:

NOTES:

WEBSITE:

USERNAME:

PASSWORD:

NOTES:

WEBSITE:

USERNAME:

PASSWORD:

NOTES:

WEBSITE:

USERNAME:

PASSWORD:

NOTES:

WEBSITE:

USERNAME:

PASSWORD:

NOTES:

WEBSITE:

USERNAME:

PASSWORD:

NOTES:

WEBSITE:

USERNAME:

PASSWORD:

NOTES:

WEBSITE:

USERNAME:

PASSWORD:

NOTES:

WEBSITE:

USERNAME:

PASSWORD:

NOTES:

WEBSITE:

USERNAME:

PASSWORD:

NOTES:

WEBSITE:

USERNAME:

PASSWORD:

NOTES:

WEBSITE:

USERNAME:

PASSWORD:

NOTES:

WEBSITE:

USERNAME:

PASSWORD:

NOTES:

WEBSITE:

USERNAME:

PASSWORD:

NOTES:

WEBSITE:

USERNAME:

PASSWORD:

NOTES:

WEBSITE:

USERNAME:

PASSWORD:

NOTES:

WEBSITE:

USERNAME:

PASSWORD:

NOTES:

WEBSITE:

USERNAME:

PASSWORD:

NOTES:

WEBSITE:

USERNAME:

PASSWORD:

NOTES:

WEBSITE:

USERNAME:

PASSWORD:

NOTES:

WEBSITE:

USERNAME:

PASSWORD:

NOTES:

WEBSITE:

USERNAME:

PASSWORD:

NOTES:

WEBSITE:

USERNAME:

PASSWORD:

NOTES:

WEBSITE:

USERNAME:

PASSWORD:

NOTES:

WEBSITE:

USERNAME:

PASSWORD:

NOTES:

WEBSITE:

USERNAME:

PASSWORD:

NOTES:

WEBSITE:

USERNAME:

PASSWORD:

NOTES:

WEBSITE:

USERNAME:

PASSWORD:

NOTES:

WEBSITE:

USERNAME:

PASSWORD:

NOTES:

WEBSITE:

USERNAME:

PASSWORD:

NOTES:

WEBSITE:

USERNAME:

PASSWORD:

NOTES:

WEBSITE:

USERNAME:

PASSWORD:

NOTES:

WEBSITE:

USERNAME:

PASSWORD:

NOTES:

WEBSITE:

USERNAME:

PASSWORD:

NOTES:

WEBSITE:

USERNAME:

PASSWORD:

NOTES:

WEBSITE:

USERNAME:

PASSWORD:

NOTES:

WEBSITE:

USERNAME:

PASSWORD:

NOTES:

WEBSITE:

USERNAME:

PASSWORD:

NOTES:

WEBSITE:

USERNAME:

PASSWORD:

NOTES:

WEBSITE:

USERNAME:

PASSWORD:

NOTES:

WEBSITE:

USERNAME:

PASSWORD:

NOTES:

WEBSITE:

USERNAME:

PASSWORD:

NOTES:

WEBSITE:

USERNAME:

PASSWORD:

NOTES: